meals in minutes™
easy desserts

RECIPES
Elinor Klivans

PHOTOGRAPHS
Tucker + Hossler

weldon**owen**

contents

30 MINUTES START TO FINISH

about this book

Today's fast-paced lifestyle makes it difficult to imagine that you can create delicious desserts quickly and without much fuss. Meals in Minutes™ *Easy Desserts* is designed to show you just how easy it can be to treat your family and friends to a simple yet elegant dessert.

The recipes in this book will inspire you to look at dessert in a new, approachable way. Recipes such as rustic Apple Bread Pudding, rich Maple Flan, and light and citrusy Lemon Pudding Cake require only 15 minutes hands-on time. Other recipes such as Roasted Figs with Crème Fraîche are ready to serve in less than 30 minutes. You will also learn to make a versatile buttery cookie dough to store in the freezer and use in multiple dessert recipes. Throughout this book, you will discover tips and suggestions on planning ahead, and keeping a well-stocked pantry. With this book you will find that desserts in every season can be delicious and effortless.

30 minutes
start to finish

italian
affogato

**Toasted Almond Gelato
(page 60),** or vanilla ice
cream, 1 pint (16 fl oz/
500 ml)

**Bittersweet or semisweet
chocolate bar,** 1

**Freshly brewed espresso
or strong coffee,** 1 cup
(8 fl oz/250 ml)

SERVES 4

1 Scoop the ice cream
Put a large scoop of gelato or ice cream into
4 individual bowls. Using a vegetable peeler, shave bits
of the chocolate over the gelato.

2 Finish the dessert
Divide the hot espresso among 4 espresso cups.
Serve the espresso alongside the bowls of gelato, inviting
diners to pour the espresso over their serving.

cook's tip

Toasted almond ice cream is
available at many supermarkets,
which is a great time-saver.
Experiment with other flavors of
ice creams or gelatos such
as chocolate or dulche de leche
to vary the flavor.

strawberries with lemon & mint

1 Prepare the strawberries
In a large bowl, toss together the strawberries, lemon zest, mint, and sugar to taste. Let stand at room temperature for 15 minutes to macerate. Spoon the strawberries into individual bowls to serve.

Strawberries, 1 lb (500 g) hulled and sliced

Lemon zest, from 1 lemon, finely grated

Fresh mint, 2 tablespoons minced

Sugar, 2–4 tablespoons

SERVES 4–6

grilled balsamic-glazed nectarines

Nectarines or peaches, 4, halved and pitted

Balsamic vinegar, ¼ cup (2 fl oz/60 ml), plus more for drizzling

Vanilla ice cream, 1 pint (16 fl oz/500 ml)

SERVES 4

1 Prepare the nectarines

Prepare a gas or charcoal grill for direct grilling over medium heat or preheat a grill pan. Brush the nectarines on both sides with some of the vinegar.

2 Grill the nectarines

Lightly oil the grill rack or grill pan. Place the nectarines, cut side down, on the grill rack. Grill, turning once and brushing 2 or 3 times with the remaining vinegar, until tender and lightly charred, 5–10 minutes, depending on the ripeness of the fruit. Transfer to individual bowls or plates, arrange scoops of ice cream alongside, drizzle with balsamic vinegar, and serve.

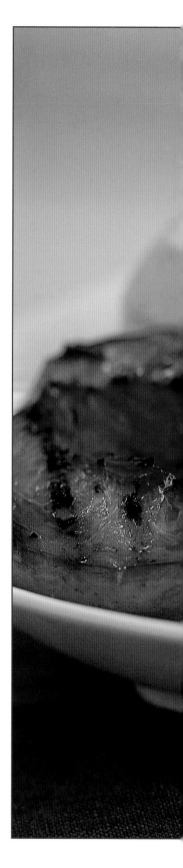

cook's tip

Grilled nectarines and peaches
not only make a simple dessert,
but are delicious served atop
grilled meats such as pork
tenderloin. You can use this
method to grill other summer
stone fruits such as plums,
pluots, or apricots.

cook's tip

You can easily put together a cheese platter with 2 or more choices. Simply vary the cheeses by milk (cow's, goat's, sheep's, or a blend),

texture (creamy to firm), and flavor (mild to strong). For example, assemble a farmhouse Cheddar, a fresh goat cheese, and a pungent blue. Serve with wedges of pear or apple and toasted almonds.

gorgonzola with walnut compote

1 **Toast the walnuts**
Remove the cheese from the refrigerator and let come to room temperature. Preheat the oven to 325°F (165°C). Spread the walnuts on a rimmed baking sheet and toast in the oven, stirring occasionally, until they have darkened slightly and are fragrant, about 10 minutes.

2 **Make the compote**
In a small saucepan over medium-low heat, combine the walnuts, dates, honey, and 2 tablespoons water until the mixture loosens, then starts to melt together, about 3 minutes. Remove from the heat. Transfer to a small bowl to cool slightly.

3 **Finish the dessert**
Core, halve, and thinly slice the apples. Arrange the cheese, apple slices, and compote on a platter and serve.

Gorgonzola *dolcelatte* or other mild blue-veined cheese, 1 wedge

Walnuts, ¼ cup (1 oz/30 g), coarsely chopped

Medjool dates, or other flavorful dates, 6, pitted and chopped

Honey, 1 tablespoon

Granny Smith apples, 2

SERVES 4

17

roasted plums with ginger & cream

Santa Rosa or other plums,
4, halved and pitted

Crystallized ginger,
2 tablespoons finely chopped

Sugar, 1 tablespoon

Whipped cream (page 79),
for serving

SERVES 4

1 **Roast the plums**
Preheat the oven to 400°F (200°C). Line a rimmed baking sheet with aluminum foil. Place the plums, cut side down and spaced at least 1 inch (2.5 cm) apart, on the prepared baking sheet. Roast the plums until just tender and their juices begin to pool, about 10 minutes, depending on their ripeness.

2 **Make the ginger syrup**
Meanwhile, in a small saucepan over medium heat, stir together the ginger, sugar, and 2 tablespoons water and bring to a gentle simmer. Cook until the flavors come together and the liquid becomes a light syrup, about 5 minutes.

3 **Finish the dessert**
Divide the hot plums among individual bowls or plates. Drizzle each serving with the ginger syrup, top with a dollop of whipped cream, and serve.

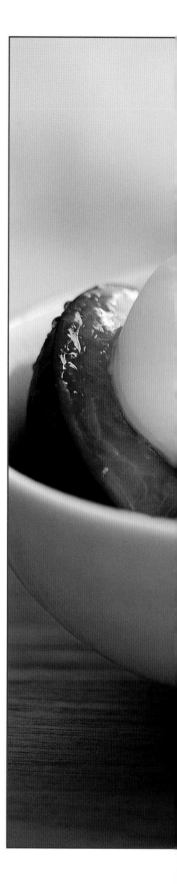

cook's tip

Purée any extra roasted plums
with a sugar syrup (see page 50)
in a blender or food processor
to make a delicious sorbet. Follow
Steps 2 and 3 on page 51
to finish and freeze the sorbet.

cook's tip

Whip the cream until it forms firm
peaks, or it will lose its volume
when you fold in the whole
berries and purée. To test if the
peaks are firm enough, lift the
beater; the peaks should be firm,
with just minimal droop at the
tips. Be careful not to over-whip,
however, or you will end up
with butter.

blackberry
fool

1 Purée the blackberries
In a food processor, purée 1 cup (4 oz/125 g) of the blackberries. Using a rubber spatula, press the purée through a fine-mesh sieve into a small bowl. Discard the seeds.

2 Whip the cream
In a large bowl, using an electric mixer on medium-high speed, beat together the cream, powdered sugar, brandy (if using), and vanilla until firm peaks form.

3 Finish the fool
Using a rubber spatula, gently fold the blackberry purée and the remaining whole blackberries into the whipped cream. Spoon the fool into glass cups or bowls and serve.

Fresh blackberries,
2¼ cups (9 oz/280 g)

Heavy (double) cream,
2 cups (16 fl oz/500 ml),
chilled

Powdered (icing) sugar,
¼ cup (1 oz/30 g)

Brandy, preferably blackberry, 1 tablespoon
(optional)

Pure vanilla extract,
1 teaspoon

SERVES 8

caramelized bananas with coconut

Unsweetened flaked or shredded dried coconut, ⅓ cup (1¼ oz/35 g)

Unsalted butter, 2 tablespoons

Light brown sugar, ½ cup (3½ oz/105 g) firmly packed

Dark rum or water, 2 tablespoons

Salt, 1 pinch

Bananas, 4, peeled and quartered lengthwise and crosswise

Vanilla or coconut ice cream, for serving

SERVES 4

1 Toast the coconut
Preheat the oven to 350°F (180°C). Spread the coconut on a rimmed baking sheet and toast in the oven, stirring occasionally, until golden, about 3 minutes. Set aside.

2 Caramelize the bananas
In a frying pan over medium heat, melt the butter. Add the brown sugar and stir to moisten with the butter. Add the rum and salt and stir to mix. Add the banana halves, cut side down. Reduce the heat to medium-low and cook, turning once, until just tender and golden, about 5 minutes total.

3 Finish the dessert
Divide the hot bananas among individual plates. Place a scoop of ice cream in the center or alongside, sprinkle with the coconut, and serve.

cook's tip

Black Mission and Turkish figs
are good varieties to use for this
dish. There are two fig seasons;
a small crop is harvested from
June through July, while a second
larger crop is in markets from
early September into October.
Look for figs with skins free
of bruises and any sign of mold.
Choose slightly underripe figs
for this dish, so they will hold their
shape during baking.

roasted figs with crème fraîche

1 Prepare the figs

Position a rack in the middle of the oven and preheat to 400°F (200°C). Butter a baking dish that will hold the figs snugly and has sides high enough to support them. Trim any tough stems from the figs and cut an X in the bottom of each fig. Arrange the figs, stem ends up, in the prepared dish.

2 Make the sauce

In a small saucepan over medium heat, combine the brown sugar, butter, and cinnamon and cook, stirring often, until the sugar dissolves and the butter melts, about 4 minutes. Pour the sauce over the figs.

3 Bake the figs

Bake until the sauce is bubbling and the figs feel soft when touched gently, 10–15 minutes. The timing will depend upon the ripeness of the figs. After 10 minutes of baking, spoon the sauce over the figs to baste. To serve, place the figs in small bowls, spoon the warm sauce over them, and serve with spoonfuls of crème fraîche.

Fresh figs, 12

Light brown sugar, ¼ cup (2 oz/60 g) firmly packed

Unsalted butter, 4 tablespoons (2 oz/60 g)

Ground cinnamon, ¼ teaspoon

Crème fraîche or sour cream, 1 cup (8 oz/250 g)

SERVES 4

pears poached in white wine

Sweet white wine such as Riesling or Muscat, 2 cups (16 fl oz/500 ml)

Sugar, ½ cup (4 oz/125 g)

Fresh ginger, 3 slices

Lemon zest, 2 wide strips

Cinnamon stick, 2-inch (5-cm) piece

Pears, 4, peeled, halved, and cored

SERVES 4

1 Poach the pears

In a wide, nonreactive saucepan over medium-high heat, combine the wine, 1 cup (8 fl oz/250 ml) water, the sugar, ginger, lemon zest, and cinnamon. Bring to a simmer, stirring often to dissolve the sugar, about 3 minutes. Add the pears, cover partially, reduce the heat to simmer, and cook at a gentle simmer until the pears are just tender when pierced with the tip of a small knife, 10–15 minutes. The timing will depend upon the ripeness of the pears.

2 Serve the pears

To serve warm, using a slotted spoon, transfer 2 pear halves to each plate. Discard the cinnamon stick and lemon peel from the syrup. Spoon some of the syrup over the pears and serve. Alternatively, pour the pears with the syrup, cinnamon stick, and lemon zest, let cool, cover, and refrigerate until well chilled, at least 5 hours.

cook's tip

A vegetable peeler or a paring knife is handy for removing long strips of citrus zest. Be careful to remove only the thin,

colored layer of the peel, leaving the bitter white pith behind. If some of the pith is attached, you can easily scrape it away with a knife. You can then cut the strips lengthwise to the width desired.

cook's tip

The raspberry sauce, known as a *coulis,* can be used to dress up a variety of desserts. Serve it over ice cream, chocolate or vanilla pudding, custard, or slices of flourless chocolate cake from your favorite bakery.

lemon mousse with raspberry sauce

1 Whip the cream
In a bowl, using an electric mixer on medium-high speed, beat 1 cup (8 fl oz/250 ml) of the cream until medium-firm peaks form, about 1 minute. Do not overwhip.

2 Make the mousse
Finely grate the zest from 1 lemon, and squeeze the juice from 2 lemons. In a large bowl, combine the ricotta, vanilla, lemon zest and juice, ¼ cup (2 oz/60 g) of the sugar, and the remaining ⅓ cup (2½ fl oz/80 ml) cream. Using the electric mixer on medium speed, beat together until smooth, adding more cream as needed for a velvety consistency. Using a rubber spatula, fold the whipped cream into the ricotta mixture.

3 Make the raspberry sauce
Squeeze 1 tablespoon juice from the third lemon. In a blender, combine two-thirds of the raspberries, the 1 tablespoon lemon juice, the remaining ¼ cup sugar, and 3 tablespoons water and process until smooth. Strain the raspberry sauce through a fine-mesh sieve into a bowl and discard the seeds. Spoon the mousse into individual bowls and drizzle generously with the raspberry sauce. Garnish with the remaining whole berries and serve.

Heavy (double) cream,
1⅓ cups (10½ fl oz/330 ml), or as needed

Lemons, 3

Whole-milk ricotta cheese,
2 cups (1 lb/500 g)

Pure vanilla extract
1 teaspoon

Sugar, ½ cup (4 oz/125 g)

Raspberries, 3 cartons, each about 6 oz (185 g)

SERVES 8

brown
sugar cookies

Unsalted butter, ¾ cup
(6 oz/185 g), at room
temperature

Salt, 1 teaspoon

Dark brown sugar, ⅔ cup
(5 oz/155 g) firmly packed

Pure vanilla extract,
1 teaspoon

Flour, 1 cup (5 oz/155 g)
plus 2 tablespoons

**Coarse sugar, such as
turbinado,** ¼ cup (2 oz/
60 g)

MAKES ABOUT
24 COOKIES

1 Mix the dough
Position 2 racks in the middle and upper third of the
oven and preheat to 350°F (180°C). Line 2 rimless baking
sheets with parchment (baking) paper. In a large bowl, using
an electric mixer on medium speed, beat together the butter,
salt, brown sugar, and vanilla until smooth. Add the flour and
mix on low speed just until evenly blended.

2 Shape the cookies
With lightly floured hands, roll the dough into 1-inch
(2.5-cm) balls and then flatten each ball into a circle. Place the
circles about 2 inches (5 cm) apart on the prepared baking
sheets. Sprinkle the top of each circle with coarse sugar.

3 Bake the cookies
Bake until the edges of the cookies darken slightly, about
12 minutes. Let the cookies cool on the pans on wire racks
for 5 minutes. Once cooled, transfer the cookies to the racks
to cool completely.

cook's tip

Make a quick citrus glaze for these cookies using 1 cup (4 oz/ 125 g) powdered (icing) sugar and 2–3 tablespoons lemon juice or water. Whisk together until smooth. The consistency can easily be altered with additional liquid if the glaze is too thick. Place the cookies on a wire rack and use a fork to drizzle the glaze over the cookies.

apple
tart

1 Prepare the puff pastry

Preheat oven to 425°F (200°C). Line a rimmed baking sheet with parchment (baking) paper. Lay the sheet of puff pastry on a very lightly floured work surface, and gently rub the top with a bit of flour. With a rolling pin, roll out into a 10-by-15-inch (25-by-38-cm) rectangle about ⅛ inch (3 mm) thick. Place the rectangle on the parchment-lined baking sheet and put in the freezer for 5 minutes while you prepare the apples.

2 Assemble the tart

Core the apples, cut them in half lengthwise, and slice into very thin half moons. With a sharp paring knife, cut a 1-inch (2.5 cm) border along the edges of the puff pastry, being careful not to cut more than halfway through the pastry. Prick the inside of the border all over with a fork, then sprinkle evenly with half of the sugar. Arrange the apple slices, slightly overlapping, on the inside of the puff pastry and sprinkle evenly with the remaining sugar.

3 Bake the tart

Bake until the puff pastry is golden brown and the apples are tender, 15–20 minutes. Cut into pieces and serve warm or at room temperature.

Frozen puff pastry, 1 sheet, thawed in the refrigerator overnight

Granny smith apples, 2

Sugar, ¼ cup

SERVES 6–8

15 minutes
hands-on time

coconut rice
pudding

Eggs, 4

Milk, 1²⁄₃ cups (13 fl oz/
410 ml)

Light brown sugar, ½ cup
(3½ oz/105 g) firmly packed

Ground cinnamon,
1 teaspoon

Salt, ⅛ teaspoon

Pure vanilla extract,
1 teaspoon

Long grain white rice,
1½ cups (10½ oz/330 g)

**Sweetened shredded
dried coconut,** ²⁄₃ cup
(2½ oz/75 g), plus toasted
coconut for serving if desired
(see page 22)

Mango, 1 large, peeled,
pitted, and sliced

SERVES 8

1 Combine the ingredients
Position a rack in the middle of the oven and preheat
to 325°F (165°C). Butter a 2-qt (2-l) baking dish. In a large
bowl, whisk together the eggs, milk, sugar, cinnamon, salt,
and vanilla. Stir in the rice and coconut. Pour the mixture
into the prepared dish.

2 Bake the pudding
Bake until the custard is set and lightly browned,
45–50 minutes. Transfer to a wire rack and let cool completely.
Serve at room temperature or refrigerate to chill slightly.
Spoon into bowls, accompany with the sliced mango, and
sprinkle with toasted coconut, if using.

cook's tip

To slice a mango neatly, stand the fruit on its side on a cutting board. Using a long, sharp knife, slice lengthwise slightly off-center (so you just graze the large pit), cutting off all the flesh from one side of the pit in a single large piece. Repeat on the other side of the pit. Carefully peel away the skin from each piece and then slice the flesh.

cook's tip

Dress up this simple chocolate
mousse by serving it in prebaked
tartlet shells. Or, fill prepared
individual chocolate cups with
the mousse and top with
whipped cream (page 79).

chocolate
mocha mousse

1 Melt the chocolate

Put the chocolate in the top of a double boiler and place it over (but not touching) barely simmering water. Heat, stirring often, until the chocolate melts. Scrape the melted chocolate into a large bowl and set aside.

2 Whip the cream

In a large bowl, using an electric mixer on medium-high speed, beat the together the cream, powdered sugar, instant coffee, and vanilla until firm peaks form.

3 Finish the mousse

Whisk about one-third of the whipped cream into the chocolate until smooth. Using a rubber spatula, fold the remaining whipped cream into the chocolate mixture. Divide the mousse between individual goblets or bowls. Cover and refrigerate for at least 2 hours or up to overnight. Serve cold.

Semisweet (plain) chocolate, 10 oz (315 g), finely chopped

Heavy (double) cream, 1½ cups (12 fl oz/375 ml), chilled

Powdered (icing) sugar, ⅔ cup (2½ oz/75 g)

Instant coffee powder, 1 tablespoon

Pure vanilla extract, 1 teaspoon

SERVES 6

apple bread pudding

Challah or other egg bread, 4 thick slices, day-old, cut into ½-inch (12-mm) cubes (about 4 cups/ 8 oz/250 g)

Dried apples, 1 cup (4 oz/ 125 g), roughly chopped

Dried currants or raisins, 2 tablespoons

Half-and-half (half cream), 1½ cups (12 fl oz/375 ml)

Eggs, 2

Light brown sugar, ¼ cup (2 oz/60 g) firmly packed

Pure vanilla extract, 1 teaspoon

Ground cinnamon, 3 teaspoons

Ground nutmeg, 1 pinch

Granulated sugar, 1 tablespoon

SERVES 6

1 Put the bread and fruits in the pan
Position a rack in the middle of the oven and preheat to 325°F (165°C). Butter a 9-by-13-by-2-inch (23-by-33-by-5-cm) baking dish. Scatter the bread cubes evenly in the prepared dish. Top evenly with the apples and currants.

2 Mix the custard
In a large bowl, whisk together the half-and-half, eggs, brown sugar, vanilla, 2 teaspoons of the cinnamon, and the nutmeg until smooth. Slowly pour the custard mixture over the bread and fruits.

3 Bake the bread pudding
In a small bowl, stir together the remaining 1 teaspoon cinnamon and the granulated sugar. Sprinkle the cinnamon-sugar mixture evenly over the pudding. Bake until the top is lightly browned and the bread cubes on the top are crisp, about 1 hour. Remove from the oven, let cool for about 20 minutes, and serve warm.

cook's tip

A simple bread pudding is the
foundation for many different
flavors. Substitute dried cherries
or apricots for the dried apples.
Or, omit the apples, currants,
cinnamon, and nutmeg and add
1 cup (6 oz/185 g) semi-sweet
chocolate chips.

cook's tip

Look for a cantaloupe with even netting on the skin and no soft spots. A ripe cantaloupe will have a sweet smell, and the stem end will give slightly when pressed. If you can find only an underripe melon, place it in a paper bag on your countertop for 2 or 3 days. It will sweeten slightly, although the sweetness won't match that of a vine-ripened cantaloupe.

cantaloupe
granita

1 Make the sugar syrup

In a small, heavy saucepan over medium-high heat, combine the sugar with ½ cup (4 fl oz/125 ml) water and heat, stirring occasionally, until the sugar dissolves, about 3 minutes. Remove from the heat, pour into a heatproof bowl, and stir in the ice cubes. Continue stirring until the sugar syrup is cold, about 1 minute. Discard any ice that is not melted. You will have about 1¼ cups (10 fl oz/310 ml) sugar syrup.

2 Make the granita base

In a food processor, combine the cantaloupe, lemon juice, and sugar syrup. Pulse a few times until the cantaloupe is broken up, and then process until a smooth purée forms, about 1 minute.

3 Freeze the granita

Pour the cantaloupe mixture into a 9-inch (23-cm) square stainless-steel pan or heavy glass dish. Freeze until the mixture is just frozen, about 1 hour. Using a fork, stir the granita to break up the ice crystals into clumps with a slushy texture. Return to the freezer and freeze until firm, but not solid, up to 1 hour. Spoon into individual glasses or bowls and serve immediately.

Sugar, ½ cup (4 oz/125 g)

Ice cubes, 10

Cantaloupe, 1, peeled, seeded, and cut into pieces (about 4 cups/1½ lb/750 g)

Fresh lemon juice, 3 tablespoons

SERVES 8

43

oatmeal-jam squares

Flour, 1½ cups (7½ oz/ 235 g)

Old-fashioned rolled oats, 1½ cups (4½ oz/140 g)

Powdered (icing) sugar, ¼ cup (1 oz/30 g)

Light brown sugar, ¾ cup (6 oz/185 g) firmly packed

Ground cinnamon, ½ teaspoon

Unsalted butter, ¾ cup (6 oz/185 g) cold, cut into ½-inch (12-mm) pieces

Apricot or other seedless fruit jam, 1 cup (10 oz/ 315 g)

MAKES ABOUT 25 SQUARES

1 Mix the crust and topping

Position a rack in the middle of the oven and preheat to 325°F (165°C). Line a 9-inch (23-cm) square baking pan with heavy-duty aluminum foil, letting the foil extend over the rim of the pan. Butter the foil. In a food processor, combine the flour, oats, powdered sugar, brown sugar, and cinnamon. Add the butter and pulse until the mixture forms fine crumbs.

2 Assemble the crust and topping

Remove 2 cups (10 oz/315 g) of the flour mixture and set aside. Transfer the remaining mixture to the prepared pan and press it evenly over the bottom and 1 inch (2.5 cm) up the sides. Drop spoonfuls of the jam evenly over the crust. Using the back of the spoon, spread the jam evenly to the edges. Don't worry if a few spots remain uncovered. The jam will spread during baking. Sprinkle the reserved flour mixture evenly over the jam.

3 Bake the squares

Bake until the edges are lightly browned and the jam filling is just beginning to bubble, about 30 minutes. Let cool completely in the pan on a wire rack. Using the ends of the foil liner, lift the square from the baking pan and place it on a cutting board. Using a sharp knife, cut into squares.

cook's tip

Lining the baking pan with buttered aluminum foil or parchment (baking) paper makes it easy to remove the baked square from the

pan, allowing you to cut it evenly into small squares. It also speeds cleanup. You can use this technique for baking a variety of other squares and bars.

cherry clafoutis

1 Prepare the cherries

Put the cherries in a bowl and add the kirsch. Stir gently to coat. Let stand for 5 minutes. Position a rack in the middle of the oven and preheat to 375°F (190°C). Butter six 1-cup (8–fl oz/250-ml) ramekins or ceramic baking dishes.

2 Assemble the clafoutis

While the cherries are soaking, in a bowl, sift together the flour, granulated sugar, and salt. Whisk in the milk and eggs until a smooth batter forms. Whisk in the vanilla. Spread the cherries evenly in the prepared ramekins. Whisk any brandy remaining in the bowl into the batter. Slowly pour the batter over the cherries, being careful not to dislodge them.

3 Bake the clafoutis

Bake until the clafoutis are puffed, the edges are browned, and the centers are lightly browned, about 30 minutes. Immediately dust with the powdered sugar shaken through a sieve, and serve.

Jarred, pitted sour cherries, 1 cup (6 oz/185 g)

Kirsch or brandy, 2 tablespoons

Flour, ¼ cup (1½ oz/45 g)

Granulated sugar, ½ cup (4 oz/125 g)

Salt, 1 pinch

Milk, 1 cup (8 fl oz/250 ml)

Eggs, 4

Pure vanilla extract, 1 teaspoon

Powdered (icing) sugar, for dusting

SERVES 6

dark chocolate pudding

Milk, 2 cups (16 fl oz/ 500 ml)

Egg yolks, 6

Sugar, ¾ cup (6 oz/185 g)

Flour, 3 tablespoons

Unsweetened cocoa powder, 2 tablespoons

Semisweet (plain) chocolate, 6 oz (185 g), finely chopped

Unsweetened chocolate, 2 oz (30 g), finely chopped

Pure vanilla extract, 1 teaspoon

Whipped cream (page 79), for serving (optional)

SERVES 6

1 Warm the milk

In a heavy saucepan over medium heat, warm the milk until a few bubbles appear along the edge of the pan. Remove from the heat.

2 Cook the pudding

In a bowl, whisk together the egg yolks and sugar until smooth. Sift together the flour and cocoa powder over the yolk mixture and whisk until smooth. While whisking constantly, slowly pour in the hot milk. Return the mixture to the pan over medium heat and cook, stirring constantly with a wooden spoon, until the mixture comes to a boil and thickens, about 4 minutes. Reduce the heat to low and cook, stirring constantly, for 1 minute.

3 Finish the pudding

Pour the pudding through a fine-mesh sieve into a bowl. Immediately add the semisweet and unsweetened chocolates and stir until melted. Stir in the vanilla. Pour into 6 individual serving bowls or glasses. Refrigerate until cold, about 2 hours. Serve with dollops of whipped cream, if desired.

cook's tip

Transform the chocolate pudding into an easy, elegant parfait by topping with layers of whipped cream and crushed chocolate wafer cookies or raspberries.

cook's tip

A sorbet base is a combination
of sugar syrup and fresh fruit or
juice. Since ripe fruits are naturally
sweet, a sugar syrup made with
2 parts sugar to 3 parts water
is usually a good ratio. Adding
liqueur, such as *framboise,*
to a raspberry sorbet base, adds
flavor. It also gives the sorbet
a creamier texture because the
alcohol lowers the freezing
temperature slightly.

plum
sorbet

1 Make the sugar syrup

In a medium saucepan over medium heat, combine ¾ cup (6 fl oz/180 ml) water and the sugar and heat, stirring occasionally, until the sugar dissolves and the syrup just comes to a boil. Pour into a small bowl, cover, and refrigerate until well chilled, at least 3 hours.

2 Prepare and churn the sorbet mixture

In a food processor, combine the chilled sugar syrup, plums, lemon juice, and brandy and process until a smooth purée forms, about 1 minute. Strain through a fine-mesh sieve into a bowl. Transfer to an ice-cream maker and process according to the manufacturer's directions.

3 Freeze the sorbet

Transfer the sorbet to an airtight container, press a layer of plastic wrap onto the surface to help keep the freshness, and freeze until firm, at least 2 hours or up to 5 days. Let soften at room temperature for about 10 minutes before serving.

Sugar, 1 cup (8 oz/250 g)

Ripe plums, 2 lb (1 kg), halved and pitted

Fresh lemon juice, ¼ cup (2 fl oz/60 ml)

Brandy, preferably plum, ¼ cup (2 fl oz/60 ml)

MAKES ABOUT 1 QUART (32 FL OZ/1 L)

chocolate-raspberry brownies

Unsalted butter, ½ cup (4 oz/125 g)

Unsweetened chocolate, 4 oz (125 g), finely chopped

Eggs, 3

Sugar, 1½ cups (12 oz/375 g)

Salt, ¼ teaspoon

Pure vanilla extract, 1 teaspoon

Flour, ¾ cup (4 oz/125 g)

Seedless raspberry jam or preserves, ½ cup (5 oz/155 g)

MAKES ABOUT
16 BROWNIES

1 **Melt the butter and chocolate**
Position a rack in the middle of the oven and preheat to 325°F (165°C). Butter a 9-inch (23-cm) square baking pan. In a small, heavy saucepan over low heat, combine the butter and chocolate and heat, stirring often, just until melted. Remove from the heat and let cool slightly.

2 **Mix the batter**
In a large bowl, whisk together the eggs, sugar, salt, and vanilla until blended. Whisk in the chocolate mixture until completely blended. Add the flour and whisk just to incorporate. Pour the batter into the prepared pan, spreading it evenly with a rubber spatula. Spoon the raspberry jam in dollops over the batter, then run a knife through the batter a few times to achieve a marbled effect.

3 **Bake the brownies**
Bake until a toothpick inserted into the center of the brownies comes out with a few moist crumbs still clinging to it, about 30 minutes. Let cool completely in the pan on a wire rack. Using a sharp knife, cut into squares and serve.

cook's tip

To add variety to your
brownies, you can try swirling
creamy peanut butter or
sweetened cream cheese that
has been loosened with
a bit of cream in place of the
raspberry jam in Step 2.

cook's tip

To peel oranges quickly, place each orange on a cutting board and cut a slice off the top and bottom, revealing the

flesh. Stand the orange upright and, using a sharp knife and following the contour of the fruit, thickly slice off the peel, cutting off both the white pith and the membrane.

caramel oranges with mascarpone

1 Cook the caramel syrup

In a heavy saucepan over medium-low heat, combine ½ cup (4 fl oz/125 ml) cold water and the granulated sugar. Cover and cook until the sugar dissolves, about 3 minutes. Uncover, raise the heat to medium-high, and bring to a boil. Cook, without stirring, until the sugar melts, caramelizes, and turns a deep gold, about 6 minutes. It is okay to swirl the pan gently to help the sugar melt evenly. Remove from the heat. Be careful, as the mixture will steam and bubble.

2 Chill the oranges

Arrange the orange slices in a bowl. Pour the warm syrup over the oranges and stir gently to coat the oranges evenly. Cover and refrigerate until cold, at least 2 hours or up to overnight.

3 Mix the mascarpone cream

In a bowl, whisk together the mascarpone, powdered sugar, and Cointreau until well blended. Divide the orange slices among small bowls or goblets, spooning the caramel syrup over the oranges. Top with spoonfuls of the mascarpone cream and serve.

Granulated sugar, 1 ¼ cups (10 oz/315 g)

Seedless oranges, 4, peeled and cut crosswise into slices

Mascarpone cheese, ½ cup (4 oz/125 g)

Powdered (icing) sugar, 1 tablespoon

Cointreau or other orange liqueur, 1 tablespoon

SERVES 4

55

frozen chai

Milk, 4 cups (32 fl oz/1l)

Chai tea, 4 tea bags

Peppercorns, 10

Fresh ginger, 3 slices

Sugar, 2 tablespoons

Vanilla ice cream, 1 pint (16 fl oz/500 ml), softened

Whipped cream (page 79), for serving (optional)

Ground cinnamon, for garnish (optional)

SERVES 4

1 Make the chai

In a medium saucepan over medium-high heat, warm the milk just until steam begins to rise. Remove from the heat and add the tea bags, peppercorns, ginger, and sugar. Stir briefly to dissolve the sugar. Let cool to room temperature, then transfer to an airtight container and chill for at least 2 hours or up to overnight.

2 Blend the chai and ice cream

Pour the chai through a fine-mesh sieve into a blender. Add the ice cream and process until smooth. Pour into individual glasses. Top with dollops of whipped cream and cinnamon, if using, and serve.

cook's tip

To chill the tea mixture quickly,
place it in a measuring cup
or small bowl and nest it inside
of a larger bowl filled with ice.
Stir the mixture occasionally
to hasten the cooling.

cook's tip

You can make a variety of truffles using this method. Instead of rolling the truffles in the spicy cocoa mixture, try rolling them in chopped toasted hazelnuts (filberts) or almonds. Or, mix in ¼ cup (2 fl oz/60 ml) bourbon with the vanilla in Step 2 and serve after dinner.

spicy chocolate truffles

1 Make the truffle filling

In a saucepan over medium heat, warm the cream and butter until the butter melts. Remove from the heat, add the semisweet and unsweetened chocolates, and let stand until softened, about 1 minute. Add the vanilla and stir until smooth. Scrape the truffle mixture into a large bowl, press a piece of plastic wrap directly onto the surface, and refrigerate until firm throughout, at least 2 hours or up to overnight.

2 Shape the truffles

On a dinner plate, using a fork, stir together the cocoa powder, sugar, chile, and cinnamon. To form each truffle, scoop up a tablespoon of the cold filling, quickly roll it between your palms into a rough ball, and roll the ball in the cocoa mixture to coat evenly. As the truffles are formed, place them on a lined baking sheet. The truffles may be served right away, or covered and refrigerated for up to 3 days. For best results, bring to room temperature before serving.

Heavy (double) cream,
¾ cup (6 fl oz/180 ml)

Unsalted butter,
2 tablespoons, at room temperature

Semisweet (plain) chocolate, 12 oz (375 g), finely chopped

Unsweetened chocolate,
1 oz (30 g), finely chopped

Pure vanilla extract,
1 teaspoon

Unsweetened cocoa powder, 3 tablespoons

Sugar, 2 tablespoons

Ground red chile,
1 tablespoon

Ground cinnamon,
1 teaspoon

MAKES ABOUT
30 TRUFFLES

toasted almond gelato

Whole milk, 1½ cups (12 fl oz/375 ml)

Heavy (double) cream, 1½ cups (12 fl oz/375 ml)

Slivered almonds, 2 cups (9 oz/270 g), toasted

Egg yolks, 5

Granulated sugar, ⅓ cup (3 oz/90 g)

Light brown sugar, ⅓ cup (2½ oz/75 g) firmly packed

MAKES ABOUT
1 QUART (32 FL OZ/
1 L)

1 Infuse the milk and cream
In a heavy saucepan over medium heat, warm the milk, cream, and almonds until a few bubbles appear along the edge of the pan. Remove from the heat and set aside to steep for at least 15 minutes. Pour through a fine-mesh sieve into a liquid measuring pitcher.

2 Prepare the custard
In a large bowl, whisk together the egg yolks and granulated and brown sugars until fluffy and lightened in color, about 3–4 minutes. While whisking constantly, pour the milk mixture into the egg yolk mixture. Return the mixture to the pan over medium-low heat and cook, stirring constantly, until the custard thickens slightly and reaches 170°F (77°C) on an instant-read thermometer, about 5 minutes. Do not let the custard boil. Pour into a bowl, let cool, cover, and refrigerate until very cold, at least 5 hours or up to overnight.

3 Churn and freeze the ice cream
Transfer the custard to an ice-cream maker and process according to the manufacturer's directions. Transfer the ice cream to an airtight container, press a layer of plastic wrap onto the surface, and freeze until firm, at least 2 hours. Let soften slightly before serving.

cook's tip

Lining the baking pan prevents the cranberries and glaze from sticking to the pan. Fold a piece of parchment (baking) paper

larger than the pan into quarters, position the point of the folded paper in the center of the pan, and press the paper into the pan so that it creases where the bottom meets the sides. Cut the paper along the crease, unfold, and press into the bottom of the pan.

cranberry upside-down cake

1 Prepare the glaze

Position a rack in the middle of the oven and preheat to 350°F (180°C). Butter a 9-inch (23-cm) round cake pan. Line the bottom of the pan with parchment (baking) paper and butter the paper. In a saucepan over medium-low heat, melt together the butter and brown sugar, stirring until smooth. Scrape the glaze into the prepared pan, tilting the pan to spread it evenly. Arrange the cranberries evenly over the glaze.

2 Make the batter

Sift together the flour, baking powder, baking soda, and salt into a bowl. In a large bowl, using an electric mixer on medium speed, beat together the egg and granulated sugar until fluffy and lightened in color, about 2 minutes. On low speed, slowly add the oil and vanilla and beat until blended. Mix in the sour cream just until no white streaks remain. Mix in the flour mixture until incorporated. Carefully pour the batter over the cranberries, spreading it evenly with a rubber spatula.

3 Bake the cake

Bake until a toothpick inserted into the center comes out clean, about 45 minutes. Let cool in the pan on a wire rack for 10 minutes. Run a thin-bladed knife around the edge of the pan, invert a serving plate on the pan, and invert both the plate and pan. Lift off the pan, being careful not to burn yourself, and carefully peel off the parchment paper. Cut into wedges and serve warm or at room temperature.

Unsalted butter,
4 tablespoons (2 oz/60 g)

Light brown sugar, ¾ cup
(6 oz/185 g) firmly packed

Fresh, or thawed frozen cranberries, 2 cups
(8 oz/250 g)

Flour, 1¼ cups
(6½ oz/200 g)

Baking powder, ½ teaspoon

Baking soda (bicarbonate of soda), ¼ teaspoon

Salt, ¼ teaspoon

Egg, 1

Granulated sugar, 1 cup
(8 oz/250 g)

Canola oil, ½ cup
(4 fl oz/125 ml)

Pure vanilla extract,
1 teaspoon

Sour cream, ½ cup
(4 oz/125 g)

SERVES 8

pear-almond
crisps

Pears, 6, peeled, halved, cored, and cut into 1-inch (2.5-cm) pieces

Light brown sugar, ¾ cup (6 oz/185 g) plus 2 tablespoons firmly packed

Unsalted butter, 9 tablespoons (4½ oz/ 140 g), melted

Fresh lemon juice, 1 tablespoon

Flour, ⅓ cup (2 oz/60 g)

Old-fashioned rolled oats, ¼ cup (1½ oz/45 g)

Slivered almonds, ½ cup (5 oz/155 g), chopped

Ground cinnamon, ¼ teaspoon

Vanilla ice cream, 1 pint (15 fl oz/500 ml), for serving (optional)

SERVES 6

1 **Make the filling**
Position a rack in the middle of the oven and preheat to 325°F (165°). Have ready six 1-cup (8–fl oz/250-ml) ovenproof bowls or ramekins on a rimmed baking sheet. In a large bowl, stir together the pears, the 2 tablespoons brown sugar, 1 tablespoon of the melted butter, and the lemon juice. Divide evenly among the bowls or ramekins. Set aside.

2 **Make the topping**
In a bowl, stir together the flour, oats, the remaining ¾ cup brown sugar, the almonds, and the cinnamon. Stir in the remaining melted butter until you have evenly moistened crumbs. Spoon the crumb mixture evenly over the pear filling.

3 **Bake the crisps**
Bake until the pears are tender when tested with a toothpick, the juices are bubbling, and the topping is golden brown, about 35 minutes. Let cool on a wire rack. Serve warm or at room temperature with the vanilla ice cream, if desired.

cook's tip

You can substitute other seasonal fruits for the pears. Apples, rhubarb, nectarines, blueberries, and mixed berries are all good choices. You will need about 5 cups (1¼ lb/625 g) cut-up fruit or whole berries to fill the 6 baking dishes. Chopped toasted pecans or toasted, peeled, and chopped hazelnuts (filberts) are other nut options.

cook's tip

If you have an unlined copper
bowl, you can use it for whipping
the egg whites, omitting the
cream of tartar. Cooks use cream
of tartar to help stabilize beaten
egg whites, but copper interacts
chemically with egg whites to
yield much the same result. If
whipping to soft peaks, the peaks
should droop when the beaters
are lifted; if whipping to stiff
peaks, they should stand upright.

lemon
pudding cake

1 Mix the batter

Position a rack in the middle of the oven and preheat to 350°F (180°C). Have ready an 8-inch (20-cm) square baking dish and a 9-by-13-inch (23-by-33-cm) baking pan. Grate 2 teaspoons zest from the lemons and squeeze ⅓ cup (3 fl oz/80 ml) juice. In a large bowl, whisk together ¾ cup (6 oz/185 g) of the sugar, the flour, and the salt. Add the melted butter, lemon juice, lemon zest, and egg yolks and continue whisking until smooth. Whisk in the milk.

2 Beat the egg whites

In a large bowl, using an electric mixer on medium-high, beat the egg whites until foamy. Slowly add the remaining ¼ cup (2 oz/60 g) sugar and beat until the whites hold stiff, shiny peaks, about 1 minute. Be careful not to overwhip the egg whites. Using a rubber spatula, fold one-third of the egg whites into the reserved batter to lighten it. Fold in the remaining egg whites just until no white streaks remain. Pour the batter into the 8-inch baking dish.

3 Bake the cake

Place the filled baking dish into the larger pan and pour hot water into the pan to reach halfway up the sides of the dish. Bake until the top of the cake is evenly light brown and firm, about 40 minutes. There may be several small cracks on top. Remove the baking dish from the water bath and place on a wire rack to cool. Serve warm, at room temperature, or cold. Scoop out each serving with a large spoon and accompany with whipped cream, if desired.

Lemons, 2–3 large

Sugar, 1 cup (8 oz/245 g)

Flour, ¼ cup (1½ oz/45 g)

Salt, ⅛ teaspoon

Unsalted butter,
4 tablespoons (2 oz/60 g), melted

Eggs, 3, separated

Milk, 1¼ cups (10 fl oz/310 ml)

Cream of tartar, ¼ teaspoon

Whipped cream (page 79), for serving (optional)

SERVES 6

maple
flan

Pure maple syrup,
7 tablespoons (5 fl oz/
160 ml)

Whole milk, 1¾ cups
(14 fl oz/430 ml)

Eggs, 2 whole, plus 2 yolks

Sugar, ⅓ cup (3 oz/90 g)

Pure vanilla extract,
1 teaspoon

Salt, ⅛ teaspoon

SERVES 6

1 Prepare the ramekins

Position a rack in the middle of the oven and preheat to 325°F (165°C). Line a shallow baking pan with a small kitchen towel. Pour 1 tablespoon of the maple syrup into each of six ¾-cup (6–fl oz/185-ml) ramekins or custard cups. Tilt each ramekin to spread the syrup evenly along the bottom and up the sides.

2 Make the custard

In a heavy saucepan over medium heat, warm the milk until a few bubbles appear along the edge of the pan. Remove from the heat. In a bowl, whisk together the whole eggs, egg yolks, sugar, vanilla, the remaining 1 tablespoon maple syrup, and the salt until blended. While whisking constantly, slowly pour in the hot milk. Pour the custard through a fine-mesh sieve into a pitcher. Divide the custard evenly among the ramekins.

3 Bake and chill the flan

Place the ramekins in the towel-lined roasting pan and pour hot water into the pan to reach halfway up the sides of the ramekins. Bake until the centers of the custards are set when the ramekins are given a gentle shake, about 50 minutes. Carefully transfer the pan to a wire rack. Remove the ramekins from the water bath as soon as they are cool enough to handle. Cover and refrigerate until well chilled, about 4 hours. To unmold, run a thin, sharp knife around the edge of each flan. Invert a dessert plate on top of each ramekin and invert the plate and ramekin together. Lift off the ramekins and serve. The maple syrup will form a sauce around each flan.

cook's tip

Make a spiced maple flan by incorporating freshly grated nutmeg into the mixture. Using a fine rasp grater, finely grate ¼ teaspoon nutmeg and add it to the custard along with the syrup mixture in Step 2.

nectarine-raspberry cobbler

1 Mix the filling

Position a rack in the middle of the oven and preheat to 375°F (190°C). Have ready an 8-inch (20-cm) square baking dish. In a large bowl, gently stir together the nectarines, raspberries, and 3 tablespoons of the sugar. Pour into the baking dish, spreading them evenly.

2 Mix the topping

In a small bowl, whisk together the buttermilk and vanilla. In a large bowl, mix together the flour, ¼ cup (2 oz/60 g) of the sugar, the baking powder, baking soda, and salt. Using a pastry blender or 2 knives, cut in the cold butter until the mixture forms coarse crumbs about the size of peas. Add the buttermilk mixture and stir lightly until a soft dough forms. Drop the dough by heaping spoonfuls onto the fruit, spacing it evenly. It will spread during baking. Brush the dough lightly with the melted butter, then sprinkle with the remaining 1 tablespoon sugar.

3 Bake the cobbler

Bake until the filling is bubbling gently, the topping is lightly browned, and a toothpick inserted into the center of the topping comes out clean, about 35 minutes. Let cool for about 15 minutes on a wire rack. Serve warm with the vanilla ice cream, if desired.

Nectarines, 4 (about 1½ lb/750 g total weight), halved, pitted, and sliced

Raspberries, 1 cup (4 oz/125 g)

Sugar, ½ cup (4 oz/125 g)

Buttermilk, ¾ cup (6 fl oz/ 180 ml)

Pure vanilla extract, 1 teaspoon

Flour, ¾ cup (4 oz/125 g)

Baking powder, 1 teaspoon

Baking soda (bicarbonate of soda), 1 teaspoon

Salt, ½ teaspoon

Unsalted butter, 6 tablespoons (3 oz/90 g) cold, cut into ½-inch (12-mm) pieces, plus 1 tablespoon, melted

Vanilla ice cream, for serving (optional)

SERVES 8

make more
to store

butter
cookies

BUTTER COOKIE DOUGH

All-purpose (plain) flour,
3 cups (15 oz/470 g)

Cake (soft-wheat) flour,
2¼ cups (9 oz/280 g)

Salt, 1½ teaspoons

Unsalted butter, 2¼ cups
(18 oz/560 g), at room
temperature

Powdered (icing) sugar,
1½ cups (6 oz/185 g)

Pure vanilla extract,
1 tablespoon

**Semisweet (plain)
chocolate chips,** 8 oz
(250 g)

MAKES ABOUT
30 COOKIES

makes 3 disks
cookie dough total

This easy-to-assemble recipe yields enough dough
for a batch of crumbly, rich cookies, plus a crust
for desserts such as the blueberry galette or pumpkin
or Key lime tart on the pages that follow.

1 Make the dough
Sift together the all-purpose and cake flours and the
salt into a bowl. In a large bowl, using an electric mixer on low
speed, beat together the butter, powdered sugar, and vanilla
until smooth, about 1 minute. Add the flour mixture and mix
just until a moist dough forms. Form the dough into three
equal disks and wrap separately in plastic wrap. Chill 1 disk until
firm, about 45 minutes, and store the remaining 2 disks for
future use (see Storage Tip, right).

2 Cut out the cookies
Position a rack in the middle of the oven and preheat
to 350°F (180°C). Line 2 baking sheets with parchment (baking)
paper. On a lightly floured work surface, roll out 1 dough disk
¼ inch (6 mm) inch thick. Using a 2-inch (5-cm) round cookie
cutter, cut out cookies. Transfer them to the prepared sheets,
spacing them about 1 inch (2.5-cm) apart.

3 Bake the cookies
Bake until the cookies are golden, about 15 minutes.
Transfer to a rack to cool. Meanwhile, melt the chocolate at
10-second intervals in the microwave until smooth and melted,
stirring often. Dip one half of each cookie into the chocolate
and return to the rack, allowing the chocolate to set. Store in an
airtight container at room temperature for up to 5 days.

storage tip

You may store the dough disks, wrapped tightly in plastic, in the refrigerator for up to 2 days or in the freezer for up to 1 month. Thaw in the refrigerator overnight and soften at room temperature. You may also roll out a disk, line a tart or pie pan, cover tightly with plastic wrap, and refrigerate overnight, or freeze for up to 1 month. It can go directly from the freezer to the oven.

cook's tip

This rustic tart showcases fresh, seasonal fruit. In the summer, try mixed berries or pitted and sliced nectarines, and in the winter, make use of cored and peeled apples or pears. For a fast version, omit the streusel topping. You can also roll out the crust in advance and freeze. Bring to room temperature before filling and baking.

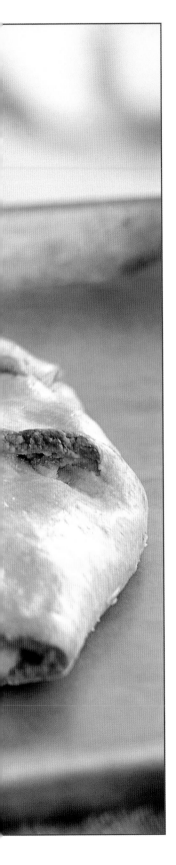

blueberry
streusel galette

1 **Roll out the dough**
Line a rimmed baking sheet with parchment (baking) paper. Put the dough disk between 2 large sheets of parchment paper and roll out into a 12-inch (30-cm) round about ¼ inch (6 mm) thick. Fold the dough round in half and transfer to the prepared baking sheet. Unfold the round; it may overlap the edges of the sheet.

2 **Prepare the filling and streusel**
Position a rack in the middle of the oven and preheat the oven to 375°F (190°C). In a large bowl, stir together the blueberries, granulated sugar, and lemon juice. Leaving a 2-inch (5-cm) border uncovered, spread the blueberry mixture over the dough round, mounding it slightly toward the center. In a bowl, stir together the flour, brown sugar, oats, and cinnamon. Add the melted butter and stir until the mixture is evenly moistened and sprinkle over the blueberries.

3 **Shape and bake the galette**
Fold the border up and over the filling, pleating it loosely around the edge and leaving the center open. Bake until the crust is golden and the fruit is bubbling, about 40 minutes. Let cool on the pan on a wire rack. Transfer to a cutting board, cut into wedges, and serve warm or at room temperature.

Butter Cookie Dough (page 74), 1 disk, at cool room temperature

Blueberries, 1½ cups (12 oz/375 g))

Granulated sugar, 2 tablespoons

Lemon juice, 1 tablespoon

Flour, ½ cup (2½ oz/75 g)

Light brown sugar, ⅓ cup (2½ oz/75 g) firmly packed

Old-fashioned rolled oats, ¼ cup (¾ oz/20 g)

Ground cinnamon, ½ teaspoon

Unsalted butter, 3 tablespoons, melted

SERVES 8

creamy
pumpkin tart

**Butter Cookie Dough
(page 74),** 1 disk, at cool
room temperature

Eggs, 2

Dark brown sugar, ¾ cup
(6 oz/185 g) firmly packed

Heavy (double) cream,
⅔ cup (5 fl oz/160 ml)

Pure vanilla extract,
1 teaspoon

Ground cinnamon,
1 teaspoon

Ground ginger,
1½ teaspoons

Salt, ¼ teaspoon

Pumpkin purée, 1 can
(15 oz/470 g)

Whipped cream (page 79),
for serving (optional)

SERVES 8

1 Partially bake the crust

Put the dough disk between 2 large sheets of parchment (baking) paper and roll out into a 12-inch (30-cm) round ¼ inch (6 mm) thick. Fold the dough round in half and transfer to a 10½-inch (26-cm) tart pan with a removable bottom. Unfold the round and ease into the pan, patting it firmly into the bottom and up the sides. Trim the edges to form a ½-inch (12-mm) overhang. Fold the overhang back over itself and press it into the sides of the pan. Freeze for at least 30 minutes or up to overnight. Preheat the oven to 375°F (190°C). Line the crust with aluminum foil and fill with pie weights, place on a baking sheet, and bake for 10 minutes. Remove the foil and weights and continue to bake until set and lightly golden, about 5 minutes. Transfer to a wire rack and reduce the oven temperature to 350°F (180°C).

2 Make the filling

In a bowl, whisk together the eggs and brown sugar until smooth. Whisk in the cream, vanilla, cinnamon, ginger, and salt until smooth, about 1 minute. Whisk in the pumpkin until blended. Pour the filling into the partially baked crust.

3 Bake the tart

Bake until the filling looks set when you give the pan a gentle shake, about 30 minutes. Transfer to a wire rack until the top feels cool to the touch, about 1 hour. Remove the tart from the pan. Serve at room temperature or refrigerate until cold. Cut the tart into wedges and serve each wedge topped with whipped cream, if desired.

cook's tip

To make whipped cream, combine 1 cup (8 fl oz/250 ml) well-chilled heavy (double) cream, 1 teaspoon pure vanilla extract, and 2 tablespoons powdered (icing) sugar in a large metal bowl. Using an electric mixer on medium-high speed, beat the cream until soft peaks form.

cook's tip

You can use a prepared graham
cracker crust for this tart as well.
Choose a 9-inch (23-cm) tart
shell and follow the recipe starting
with Step 2. Be aware that the
purchased crust may take up to
10 minutes longer to bake.

lemon tart with raspberries

1 Partially bake the crust

Put the dough disk between 2 large sheets of parchment (baking) paper and roll out into a 12-inch (30-cm) round ¼ inch (6 mm) thick. Fold the dough round in half and transfer to a 10½-inch (26-cm) tart pan with a removable bottom. Unfold the round and ease into the pan, patting it firmly into the bottom and up the sides. Trim the edges to form a ½-inch (12-mm) overhang. Fold the overhang back over itself and press it into the sides of the pan. Freeze for at least 30 minutes or up to overnight. Preheat the oven to 375°F (190°C). Line the crust with aluminum foil and fill with pie weights, place on a baking sheet, and bake for 10 minutes. Remove the foil and weights and continue to bake until set and lightly golden, about 5 minutes. Transfer to a wire rack and reduce the oven temperature to 350°F (180°C).

2 Mix the filling

In a food processor, combine the eggs and sugar and process until smooth, about 1 minute. Add the cream cheese, pulse to break it up, and then process until smooth, about 15 seconds. Add the sour cream, lemon zest and juice, flour, and vanilla and process just until smooth, about 20 seconds. Pour the filling into the partially baked crust.

3 Bake the tart

Bake until the top looks firm and is set when you gently shake the pan, about 35 minutes. Transfer to a wire rack to cool, about 1 hour. Remove the tart from the pan. Cover and refrigerate until cold, at least 3 hours or up to overnight. Spoon the raspberries on top of the tart just before serving.

Butter Cookie Dough, (page 74), 1 disk, at cool room temperature

Eggs, 2

Sugar, ⅔ cup (5 oz/155 g)

Cream cheese, 12 oz (375 g), at room temperature

Sour cream, ½ cup (4 oz/125 g)

Lemon zest, 2 teaspoons, finely grated

Lemon juice, from 1 lemon

Flour, 2 tablespoons

Pure vanilla extract, 1 teaspoon

Raspberries, 1 carton, about 6 oz (185 g)

SERVES 8

key lime custard tart

Butter Cookie Dough (page 74), 1 disk, at cool room temperature

Eggs, 2

Sugar, 1½ cups (12 oz/ 375 g)

Lime zest, preferably from Key limes, 1 teaspoon freshly grated

Fresh lime juice, preferably from Key limes, ½ cup (4 fl oz/125 ml), from 7 or 8 limes

Flour, ¼ cup (1½ oz/45 g)

Heavy (double) cream, ¼ cup (2 fl oz/60 ml)

Whipped cream (page 79), for serving (optional)

SERVES 8

1 Partially bake the crust

Put the dough disk between 2 large sheets of parchment (baking) paper and roll out into a 12-inch (30-cm) round ¼ inch (6 mm) thick. Fold the dough round in half and transfer to a 10½-inch (26-cm) tart pan with a removable bottom. Unfold the round and ease into the pan, patting it firmly into the bottom and up the sides. Trim the edges to form a ½-inch (12-mm) overhang. Fold the overhang back over itself and press it into the sides of the pan. Freeze for at least 30 minutes or up to overnight. Preheat the oven to 375°F (190°C). Line the crust with aluminum foil and fill with pie weights, place on a baking sheet, and bake for 10 minutes. Remove the foil and weights and continue to bake until set and lightly golden, about 5 minutes. Transfer to a wire rack and reduce the oven temperature to 350°F (180°C).

2 Make the filling

In a large bowl, whisk together the eggs, sugar, lime juice and zest until smooth, about 1 minute. Whisk in the flour until incorporated. Whisk in the ¼ cup cream until blended. Pour the filling into the partially baked crust.

3 Bake the tart

Bake until the filling looks set when you give the pan a gentle shake, about 30 minutes. Transfer to a wire rack until the top feels cool to the touch, about 1 hour. Remove the tart from the pan and cover and refrigerate until cold, at least 3 hours or up to overnight. Cut the tart into wedges and serve topped with whipped cream, if desired.

cook's tip

Fully baking or partially baking a crust (also known as blind baking) before adding the filling can prevent a soggy crust. Use heavy-duty aluminum foil to line it, or fold regular aluminum foil to create a double thickness. For the weights, use small ceramic or metal weights, dried beans, or rice. The crust may be cooled, covered, and stored at room temperature for up to overnight.

storage tip

You may wrap the cake tightly in plastic wrap and store it at room temperature for up to 3 days. Or, wrap the cake tightly in plastic wrap and then in aluminum foil and freeze for up to 2 months. Thaw the wrapped cake at room temperature before using.

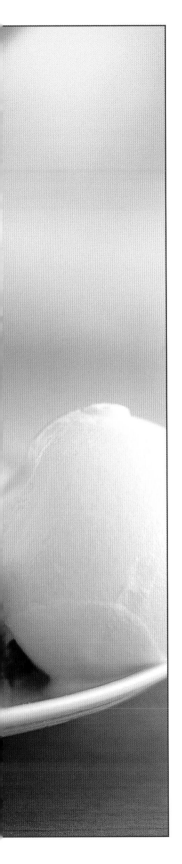

pound cake

This rich, moist pound cake can be served with seasonal fruit and ice cream, used to line a pan for an old-fashioned icebox cake, cut into chunks for a creamy trifle or ice cream parfaits, or split into layers for a cream-filled cake.

1 Sift the dry ingredients
Position a rack in the middle of the oven and preheat to 325°F (165°C). Butter two 9-by-5-inch (23-by-13-cm) loaf pans and line with buttered parchment (baking) paper. Sift together the flour, baking powder, and salt into a bowl.

2 Make the batter
In a large bowl, using an electric mixer on medium speed, beat together the butter and granulated sugar until fluffy and lightened in color, about 2 minutes. Add the eggs two at a time, beating well after each addition. Mix in the vanilla. On low speed, add half of the flour mixture and mix until incorporated. Mix in the cream until blended. Add the remaining flour mixture and mix just until a smooth batter forms. Divide the batter evenly between the prepared pans.

3 Bake the cakes
Bake until the top of each cake is golden and a toothpick inserted into the center comes out clean, about 1 hour. Briefly cool in the pans on a wire rack for about 20 minutes. Remove the cakes from the pans to cool completely. Dust the top of 1 cake with powdered sugar and slice to serve. Reserve the second cake for another dessert (see Storage Tip).

POUND CAKE

Flour, 4 cups (1 ¼ lb/625 g)

Baking powder, 1 teaspoon

Salt, ½ teaspoon

Unsalted butter, 1 lb (500 g), at room temperature

Granulated sugar, 3 cups (1 ½ lb/750 g)

Eggs, 8, lightly beaten

Pure vanilla extract, 2 teaspoons

Heavy (double) cream, ½ cup (4 fl oz/125 ml)

Powdered (icing) sugar, for dusting

MAKES TWO 9-BY-5-INCH (23-BY-13-CM) LOAF CAKES

hot fudge parfaits

Pound Cake (page 85),
1 loaf

Half-and-half (half cream),
½ cup (4 fl oz/125 ml)

Unsweetened chocolate,
4 oz (125 g), finely chopped

Sugar, ¾ cup (6 oz/185 g)

Light corn syrup,
2 tablespoons

Salt, ⅛ teaspoon

Vanilla ice cream, 1 qt (1 l),
slightly softened

SERVES 6

1 Make the fudge sauce
In a saucepan over low heat, combine the half-and-half, chocolate, sugar, corn syrup, and salt and cook, stirring constantly, until the chocolate melts and the sugar dissolves, about 4 minutes. Raise the heat to medium-low and continue cooking, stirring often, until the sauce thickens and is smooth, about 3 minutes longer.

2 Assemble the parfaits
Trim off the ends of the cake and cut the cake into small chunks. Have ready 6 tall sundae glasses or goblets. To make each parfait, spoon 1 tablespoon of the warm fudge sauce into the bottom of a glass. Top with a scoop of ice cream and spoon in pieces of the pound cake. Top with another scoop of ice cream. Spoon about 1 tablespoon fudge sauce over the ice cream. Repeat with another layer of pound cake, ice cream, and fudge sauce and then serve.

cook's tip

Make this easy dessert even
quicker by using good-quality,
purchased bittersweet chocolate
or hot fudge sauce, instead of
making your own. For a change
in flavor, add 1 tablespoon liqueur
to the fudge sauce. Try Kahlúa,
raspberry liqueur, or frangelico.

cook's tip

Any combination of berries
will work for this cake, such as
blackberries and strawberries
or boysenberries and raspberries.
You will need about 2½ cups
(10 oz/315 g) total.

mixed berry whipped cream cake

1 Make the filling

In a large bowl, using an electric mixer on medium-high speed, beat together the cream, powdered sugar, liqueur, and vanilla until stiff peaks form. Use a rubber spatula to gently fold in the raspberries and blueberries.

2 Assemble the cake

Using a large, thin-bladed serrated knife, cut the cake horizontally into 3 equal layers. Place the bottom cake layer on a serving plate and, using an icing spatula, spread with halfof the whipped cream with berries. Place the middle cake layer on top of the cream, spread with the remaining half of the whipped cream. Top with the final cake layer. Refrigerate for at least 2 hours or up to 5 hours. Just before serving, dust the top of the cake with powdered sugar shaken through a sieve. Slice, and serve.

Pound cake (page 85),
1 loaf

Heavy (double) cream,
1 cup (8 fl oz/250 ml), chilled

Powdered (icing) sugar,
¼ cup (1 oz/30 g), plus more for dusting

Raspberry liqueur,
1 tablespoon

Pure vanilla extract,
1 teaspoon

Raspberries, 1 cup
(8 oz/250 g)

Blueberries, 1 cup
(8 oz/250 g)

SERVES 8

89

cherry
trifle

Pound Cake (page 85),
1 loaf

Jarred, pitted sour cherries, 2 cups
(12 oz/375 g)

Kirsch, 5 tablespoons
(3 fl oz/80 ml)

Granulated sugar,
1 tablespoon

Heavy (double) cream,
2 cups (16 fl oz/500 ml)

Powdered (icing) sugar,
¼ cup (1 oz/30 g)

Pure vanilla extract,
1 teaspoon

SERVES 10

1 Prepare the cherries
In a bowl, gently stir together the cherries, 4 tablespoons (2 fl oz/60 ml) of the kirsch, and the granulated sugar. Let stand for 10–15 minutes. Drain the cherries through a fine-mesh sieve placed over a bowl. Reserve the liquid and cherries separately.

2 Whip the cream
In a large bowl, using an electric mixer on medium-high speed, beat together the cream, powdered sugar, the remaining 1 tablespoon kirsch, and the vanilla just until firm peaks form.

3 Assemble the trifle
Trim off the ends of the cake and cut the cake into chunks. Line the bottom of a 2½–3-qt (2.5–3-l) clear glass bowl with about one-third of the cake. Brush lightly with some the reserved cherry liquid. Spoon one-third of the cherries over the cake and spread one-third of the whipped cream over the cherries. Repeat the layering two more times, ending with whipped cream. Cover and refrigerate for at least 3 hours or up to overnight before serving. Serve cold.

cook's tip

A classic trifle often contains
pastry cream and whipped
cream. You can use good-quality
purchased vanilla pudding
instead, or make your own
from scratch. Add the pudding
layer before you add the
whipped cream.

cook's tip

Use a large sharp knife to slice
the cake. Wipe the knife clean
with a paper towel after cutting
each slice. Dipping the knife in
a glass of warm water will also
help to make neat, clean slices.
Be sure to hold the blade away
from you when wiping the knife.

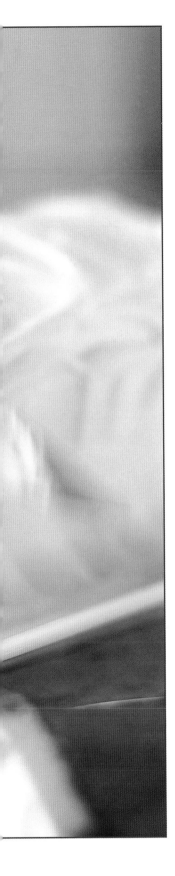

chocolate icebox cake

1 Line the pan with cake

Cut a long piece of parchment (baking) paper to fit the bottom and sides of a 9-by-5-inch (23-by-13-cm) loaf pan, including a short overhang over each end. Line the bottom and sides of the pan with the cake slices, cutting to fit as necessary. You will not use the whole cake for this recipe.

2 Make the chocolate filling

In the top pan of a double boiler, combine ½ cup (4 fl oz/125 ml) of the cream and the unsweetened and semisweet chocolates and place over (but not touching) barely simmering water. Heat, stirring often, until smooth. Remove from the heat and stir in ¼ cup (2 fl oz/60 ml) of the cold cream. Refrigerate until cool, about 10 minutes. In a large bowl, using an electric mixer on medium speed, beat the butter, powdered sugar, dissolved coffee, if using, and vanilla until smooth, about 1 minute. Mix in the chocolate mixture. In another large bowl, using the mixer on medium-high speed, beat the remaining 1½ cups cold cream until firm peaks form. Using a rubber spatula, fold half of the whipped cream into the chocolate mixture to lighten the mixture and then fold in the remaining whipped cream.

3 Assemble the cake

Spread the filling in the cake-lined pan, smoothing the top. Cover and refrigerate for at least 3 hours or up to overnight. To serve, invert a serving plate on top of the pan and invert the plate and pan together. Holding the ends of the parchment liner firmly on the plate, lift off the pan. Frost the top and sides of the cake with the whipped cream, slice, and serve.

Pound Cake (page 85), 1 loaf, ends trimmed and cut into ten ¾-inch (2-cm) slices

---

Heavy (double) cream, 2¼ cups (18 fl oz/560 ml) chilled

Unsweetened chocolate, 3 oz (90 g), finely chopped

Semisweet (plain) chocolate, 2 oz (60 g), finely chopped

Unsalted butter, ½ cup (4 oz/125 g), at room temperature

Powdered (icing) sugar, 1¼ cups (5 oz/155 g)

Instant coffee powder, ½ teaspoon, dissolved in 1 teaspoon water (optional)

Pure vanilla extract, 1 teaspoon

Whipped cream (page 79), for frosting

SERVES 10

the smarter cook

A delicious dessert is the perfect ending to nearly every meal, but many people don't think they have the time to prepare one from scratch. All the sweet treats in these pages come together quickly, and many require just 15 minutes or less of hands-on time. You'll also find savvy tips on how to dress up your creations both simply and beautifully.

It takes a little advance planning to put homemade desserts into your everyday repertoire, but the following pages explain everything you need to know. You'll learn how to keep your pantry well stocked, shop efficiently for the freshest ingredients, and plan ahead by mixing up a double batch of cookie dough and freezing some for later use. Plus, you'll find dozens of tips on how to manage your time and organize your kitchen—the keys to becoming a smarter cook.

get started

Once your pantry and cold storage are stocked with all the necessary staples (page 104–107), you'll be able to put together nearly any recipe with just a quick shopping trip to pick up fresh fruit or dairy. You'll need to give some thought to how making the recipes will fit into your busy schedule, and which desserts best suit both the season and your menus.

plan for dessert

■ **Look at the whole week.** During the weekend, take time to think about the desserts you may want to prepare in the week ahead. Is there a special event coming up—a dinner party that needs an elegant finale, or a school event where a sweet treat would be welcome? Think about what you'll serve during the week, too. A rich supper might end perfectly with a simple fruit dessert, while a casual weeknight meal might leave you with extra time to get brownies in the oven.

■ **Organize your time.** Once you've chosen what you'd like to prepare, decide when you'll have time to make it. Think about what can be made the night before or what can be frozen in advance.

■ **Get everyone involved.** Everyone loves dessert, so it's easy to enlist the help of kids or other family members in putting together a recipe. It can be as simple as peeling fruit or gathering ingredients from the pantry. Make helping out in the kitchen, from measuring ingredients to mixing batter, a special treat.

■ **Make desserts on the weekend.** Desserts fresh from the oven or just prepared always taste best, but busy weekdays seldom include time to make a tart or a batch of gelato. If possible, prepare desserts over the weekend. You can cook up a double batch of items that freeze well, such as pound cake or butter cookies, and store half in the freezer for future use. Do the time-consuming part of a recipe, like making pastry dough, when you have extra time, and chill or freeze the dough for quick desserts later in the week (see page 101 for freezing tips).

Here is a guide to using the best that each season has to offer whenever you are making dessert.

spring Celebrate the return of warm weather and the start of the growing season by showcasing early spring produce such as ripe strawberries and fragrant fresh mint.

summer The hot days of summer bring juicy stone fruits like plums, peaches, and cherries, along with ripe berries and fresh melons. Use this summertime abundance to make light, simple, appealing desserts.

autumn As the weather cools, warm up desserts with spices such as cinnamon, ginger, and nutmeg. Enjoy the seasonal bounty by preparing desserts with apples, cranberries, pears, and pumpkin.

winter With the arrival of the holidays come festive gatherings. Indulge in chocolate in all its guises, from dense mousse to rich brownies. Look for citrus and tropical fruits. Bake with year-round staples such as dried fruits, maple syrup, and fruit jams.

handling berries Fresh raspberries, blackberries, blueberries, and strawberries need gentle handling. Purchase berries close to the time you plan to serve them, and do not wash them in advance. Keep the berries in the refrigerator until you are ready to use them, and then carefully pick them over and discard any that seem to be past their prime. If you have leftover berries you can't use right away, freeze them in a single layer on a baking sheet. When they are hard, put them in a plastic freezer bag or other container and freeze for up to 6 months.

zesting & juicing citrus When a recipe calls for both citrus zest and juice, zest the fruit first. Whether the fruit is organically or conventionally grown, rinse it in warm water to remove dirt, wax, or chemicals, then pat dry. Use a Microplane grater for fine zest or a vegetable peeler for long shards of zest. Remove only the colored portion of the rind, not the bitter white pith. Halve the fruit crosswise and use a reamer or juicer to extract the juice, straining it in a fine-mesh sieve before using to remove any seeds or pulp.

working with dried fruit Removing moisture from fruit concentrates its sweetness and flavor and results in fruit that is firm and chewy. As dried fruit ages, its sugars can become crystallized; immersing the fruit in boiling water for a few minutes, however, will soften its texture. Chopping dried fruit is made easier by using a sharp knife and chilling the fruit for about 30 minutes.

dress up dessert

From a scoop of ice cream to a fresh fruit sauce, there are a number of easy additions that can turn a simple dessert into an elegant treat. Fresh fruits can be prepared a few hours ahead of time and refrigerated. High-quality ice creams and sauces are quick and delicious ways to dress up cakes and tarts, and freshly whipped cream is always a popular topping.

- **Ice cream** A small scoop of high-quality ice cream goes well with nearly every dessert, from warm bread pudding to old-fashioned fruit cobbler to simple pound cake. Choose basic flavors—vanilla, caramel, chocolate, coffee—for the most versatility.

- **Whipped cream** Real whipped cream takes only a few minutes to make, and its silky richness is unmatched by commercial products. In a chilled bowl, combine 1 cup (8 fl oz/250 ml) very cold heavy (double) cream, 2 tablespoons sugar, and ½ teaspoon pure vanilla extract. Using an electric mixer on medium-high speed, beat until medium peaks form, about 3 minutes. Use at once or cover and refrigerate until ready to serve or for up to 2 hours.

- **Fresh fruit** Top simple desserts such as pound cake with fresh raspberries, or dress berries up with a drizzle of your favorite fruit liqueur, such as Grand Marnier or framboise. Serve a plate of cookies with sliced peaches or nectarines or cubed mangoes.

- **Sauces & syrups** Good-quality chocolate, butterscotch, or caramel sauce can make simple desserts look professional. Look for a brand made from natural ingredients. Warm the sauce on the stove top or in a microwave. Drizzle it on a slice of cake or over a scoops of ice cream or gelato.

- **Easy garnishes** Use sprigs or a chiffonade of fresh mint to dress up individual servings of tart, trifle, or poached fruit. To add elegance to a plate of brownies or cookies, lightly dust it with powdered (icing) sugar using a fine-mesh sieve. Top ice cream or gelato with sweetened shredded dried coconut that has been toasted to enhance its nutty flavor. To toast coconut, spread it on a baking sheet and place in a preheated 350°F (180°C) oven until light golden brown, 8–10 minutes.

quick & easy desserts

Speed and ease characterize all of these desserts, any one of which would be welcome on a weeknight menu when you're short on time.

- **Summertime mixed-berry compote** Simmer raspberries or mixed berries, either fresh or frozen, with a cinnamon stick, or a split vanilla bean, and sugar to taste. Cook gently until syrupy, about 15 minutes. Add a little fresh lemon juice. Serve over pound cake or vanilla ice cream.

- **Sautéed autumn fruit** Sauté sliced pears and apples in a little unsalted butter and brown sugar until they start to caramelize. Mix in a generous handful of toasted chopped walnuts and raisins. Add a dash of cinnamon, if desired. Serve with a dollop of crème fraîche.

- **Ice cream sandwiches** Make quick ice cream sandwiches with purchased cookies, such as chocolate wafers with mint-chip ice cream or gingersnaps with vanilla gelato. Let the ice cream soften, spread a layer ½ inch (12 mm) thick on the bottom side of half of the cookies, top with the remaining cookies, bottom side down, and cover with plastic wrap. Freeze for at least 1 hour before serving.

- **Port & Stilton** Sweet wines can be desserts by themselves. For an easy conclusion to any meal, serve glasses of vintage-style or wood-aged port alongside a strong blue cheese such as Stilton. Remove the cheese from the refrigerator at least 1 hour before serving. It is essential that cheese be at room temperature, because cold mutes the subtle flavor.

- **Chocolate sauce** Chop dark chocolate into small pieces and melt in a saucepan over low heat. Drizzle over coffee or vanilla ice cream. Or, to make chocolate-dipped strawberries, leaving the stems intact, dip each berry into the melted chocolate, coating three-fourths of the fruit. Place on parchment (baking) paper to set and then serve.

- **Roasted or grilled stone fruit** Halve and pit nectarines or peaches and brush with honey or sprinkle with brown sugar. Roast in a hot oven or on a grill until browned and caramelized. Serve with vanilla ice cream or crème fraîche.

baking pans These come in many shapes and sizes and are usually made of tempered glass or heavy-gauge aluminum. For this book, you'll need 8-inch (20-cm) and 9-inch (23-cm) square baking pans, a 9-by-13-inch (23-by-33-cm) pan, and two loaf pans.

cake pans These round pans are generally 2 inches (5 cm) deep and 8 or 9 inches (20 or 23 cm) in diameter. You will want to have at least two on hand for making layer cakes.

baking sheets Sometimes called cookie sheets or jelly-roll pans, these large, rectangular metal pans either have a shallow rim or have one or two ends with low, flared rims for sliding cookies onto cooling racks. It's handy to have two sheets, so you can fill one sheet while the other one is in the oven. Heavy baking sheets are better, as they bake and brown cookies and other items more evenly than thinner sheets.

ramekins These single-serving, ovenproof porcelain dishes, which look like mini soufflé dishes, are useful for making individual cakes and desserts. For this book, you'll need both 3/4-cup (6–fl oz/180-ml) ramekins and 1-cup (8–fl oz/250-ml) ramekins.

tart pans Available in many sizes and shapes, shallow metal tart pans usually have fluted edges and come with a removable bottom for easy unmolding.

glass dishes Serve frozen or layered desserts in glass vessels.

easy techniques

■ **Beating** Mixing ingredients together vigorously until they are smooth and thoroughly amalgamated is called beating. It's also the term used for whipping air into heavy (double) cream or egg whites. Egg whites and cream can be beaten with a whisk, a handheld mixer, or the whip attachment of a stand mixer.

■ **Cutting in** Recipes for everything from flaky pastry dough to biscuity cobbler topping often call for cutting chilled butter into the flour mixture. To cut in the butter, chop it into cubes. If making the dough by hand, cut the butter into the flour using a pastry blender or two table knives. The mixture should be coarse, with pea-sized pieces of butter. If using a food processor, pulse the cold butter into the flour in short bursts, until the same consistency is reached.

■ **Creaming** Beating softened, but not melted, butter with sugar or other ingredients is called creaming. This process mixes air into the butter, which helps the mixture rise when baked. It also blends the sugar into the butter, forming a smooth mixture. Beat the butter with a wooden spoon, a handheld mixer, or the paddle attachment of a stand mixer for several minutes until creamy. Gradually add the sugar and beat for a few minutes until fluffy.

■ **Melting chocolate** To melt chocolate, chop it into small chunks and place it in the top pan of a double boiler or a heatproof bowl set over barely simmering water. Make sure the water does not touch the bottom of the top pan, and do not let the water boil. Moisture or steam that comes in contact with the chocolate could cause it to seize, or stiffen. As it melts, stir the chocolate with a wooden spoon. When the chocolate is liquefied, remove the top of the double boiler from the bottom. To melt chocolate in a microwave, place the chunks in a microwave-safe dish and heat on low. Stir it after 1 minute and check on it every 30 or 40 seconds thereafter to make sure it doesn't scorch. When the chocolate is shiny and soft, remove it. Although it will not be completely melted, it will become smooth and flowing when you stir it.

make the most of your time

Once you've made a plan for which desserts to make in the week ahead, give some thought to how you will organize your time. Do as many tasks as you can in advance, so that your desserts come together quickly—even on busy weeknights.

▪ **Stock up.** Over the weekend, check the pantry and refrigerator for the staples you'll need during the week. If you replace basic ingredients soon after you use them, you'll always be able to improvise a quick and easy dessert, such as those suggested on page 98.

▪ **Shop less.** With a plan for the week's desserts in place, you won't need to shop as often. In the summer, you might plan a couple of quick shopping trips to pick up berries or other perishable items. If you are making desserts with autumn fruits that store well, such as apples or pears, you may need to shop for produce just once during the week.

▪ **Do it ahead.** Do as much as you can ahead of time. For example, gather ingredients in the morning to save time in the evening. Planning in advance will help you efficiently accomplish time-consuming steps such as chilling, an essential step in such recipes as mousse and flan. Remember, too, that sorbet, gelato, and other frozen desserts can be made a day ahead and stored in the freezer, leaving you with minimal work to do at dinnertime.

▪ **Double up.** The master recipes for Butter Cookies and Pound Cake in Chapter 3, Make More to Store (pages 74 and 85), are designed to yield double batches so you can reserve the second batch for another day. This approach works well with other cookie and cake recipes, too.

▪ **Cook smarter.** Before you begin, reread the recipe carefully. As you review it, take note of any time-saving steps, such as making ginger syrup on the stove top while the accompanying plums roast in the oven (page 18) or chilling the puff pastry for an apple tart in the freezer while you prepare the fruit (page 33). Then, do as professional chefs do and assemble, prep, and measure all the ingredients you'll need. Get out all the equipment required at the same time, so everything is ready to go.

MAKE A SHOPPING LIST

prepare in advance Create your shopping list after planning your weekly desserts. Review the recipes while you assemble the list, so you know exactly what you will need. Check the pantry as well as your cold storage area (see lists of staples, pages 106 and 107) before making your list.

make a template Create a list template on your computer, then fill it in during the week before you go shopping.

categorize your lists Use the following categories to keep your lists organized: pantry, fresh, and occasional.

▪ **pantry items** Check the pantry and write down any items that need to be restocked to make the desserts on your weekly plan.

▪ **fresh ingredients** These are for immediate use and include most fresh fruits and some cheeses. You might need to visit different supermarket or store sections, so divide the list into subcategories, such as produce and dairy. Precut fresh fruits, such as melon or pineapple, are often available and can save time, but whole fresh fruits you cut yourself will yield much better flavor.

▪ **occasional items** This is a revolving list for refrigerated items that are replaced as needed, such as milk, cream, butter, cheese, and eggs.

▪ **be flexible** Be ready to change your dessert choice based on the freshest ingredients at the market.

cakes & brownies are done when a wooden toothpick inserted into the center comes out clean. The center should spring back when pressed lightly with a fingertip, and the edges of the cake or bread should have pulled away from the sides of the pan.

pie & tart pastry should be golden brown. Fruit fillings should be bubbly and juicy, while custard fillings should be set when you gently shake the pan.

cookies should generally be firm and lightly browned around the edges. Always check recipes for specific tips on testing doneness.

COOLING BAKED GOODS

Always cool baked goods on a footed wire rack, which allows air to circulate on all sides. The items will cool faster and they are less likely to become soggy.

For cakes, let cool in the pan for about 10 minutes or as instructed by the recipe, then, if necessary, loosen the edges with a table knife. Place the wire rack upside down on top of the cake. Using pot holders, invert the pan and the rack and shake gently to unmold the cake onto the rack. Cool tarts, cobblers, and pies in their pans on a rack.

To cool most cookies, transfer them from the baking sheet to the rack with a spatula, or slide them from the rimless end of a cookie sheet onto the rack.

dessert storage

Frozen desserts, such as sorbet and gelato, must be stored in the freezer. Most baked goods can be stored at room temperature in airtight containers or plastic wrap for a couple of days. Some items require refrigeration, however, or can be frozen for longer storage. Desserts such as tarts and pies may be made in advance and refrigerated, but remember to bring to room temperature before serving.

Freezing cakes & cookies To store undecorated cookies and unfrosted cakes for more than a couple of days, freeze them. Let them cool completely after baking, then wrap tightly in aluminum foil, plastic wrap, or freezer paper. Store small items like cookies and muffins in resealable plastic freezer bags. Thaw at room temperature or in the refrigerator. To serve them, warm in the oven at 250°F (120°C) until heated through.

Storing tart & pie dough Store unbaked disks of tart and pie dough, tightly wrapped or in a resealable plastic bag, in the refrigerator for up to 3 days. To freeze disks of dough or unbaked lined pie or tart shells, wrap in aluminum foil or plastic wrap and freeze for up to 4 months. Frozen shells can go directly from the freezer to the oven without thawing.

Refrigerating pies, tarts & cakes In general, pies and tarts with custard-based fillings, such as pumpkin pie, do not freeze well. Once they are made, store them in the refrigerator. Refrigerate cakes with whipped cream frostings immediately and serve them chilled.

Storing ice cream, sorbet & gelato Generally, freshly made ice cream, gelato, and sorbet should be put in the freezer for at least 2 hours, or until firm, before serving. Store in an airtight container and press plastic wrap directly onto the surface of the ice cream, gelato or sorbet to preserve freshness. Store in the freezer for up to 5 days, and let soften at room temperature for about 10 minutes before serving.

Storing puff pastry Frozen commercial puff pastry is an excellent alternative to making the pastry yourself. Thaw the frozen puff pastry in the refrigerator according to the package instructions and keep it chilled until ready to use.

the well-stocked kitchen

Smart cooking is about being prepared. Keeping your pantry, refrigerator, and freezer well stocked and organized means you won't have to run to the store at the last minute. Get into the habit of keeping track of what's in your kitchen, and you'll find you can shop less frequently and spend less time in the store when you do.

On the pages that follow, you'll find a guide to the essential ingredients to have on hand for making the recipes in this book as well as your other favorite desserts. You'll also find tips on how to keep these ingredients fresh and store them efficiently. Use this guide to stock your kitchen now and you'll be able to make any recipe in this book by picking up just a few fresh ingredients on a quick shopping trip.

the pantry

The pantry is typically a closet or one or more cupboards in which you store flour, sugar, dried spices, extracts and other flavorings, dried fruits, nuts, and canned and bottled or jarred foods. Make sure that it is relatively cool, dry, and dark when not in use. It should also be a good distance from the stove, as heat can dry out pantry staples, especially spices, robbing them of their flavor and aroma.

pantry storage

- **Spices & flavorings** The flavor of dried spices starts to fade after about 6 months. Buy spices in small quantities so you can use them up, and replace them often. Ethnic markets and natural-foods stores usually sell spices in bulk. They are typically fresher and much less expensive than the prepackaged spices on supermarket shelves. For flavorings and extracts, buy the highest quality you can afford, and avoid artificial or imitation products. Store them in airtight containers in a cool, dry place, away from the heat of the stove.

- **Nuts & dried fruits** Store most nuts and all dried fruits in airtight containers for up to 1 month. To keep them longer, refrigerate them for up to 6 months, or freeze them for up to 9 months.

- **Chocolate & cocoa** Buy the best-quality chocolate and cocoa powder that you can afford. Unsweetened chocolate, which is also known as baking chocolate, contains no sugar and is hard and extremely bitter. Bittersweet and semisweet (plain) chocolate have some sugar and cocoa butter added, making them smoother and sweeter. They are not interchangeable with unsweetened chocolate. To store chocolate, wrap it in aluminum foil and plastic wrap; it will keep for up to 1 year. Temperature fluctuations can cause chocolate to develop a chalky white film, sometimes referred to as "bloom." Although the chocolate will look less appealing, its quality is unaffected, and the color disappears as soon as the chocolate is melted. Always use unsweetened cocoa powder, not hot-cocoa mix, for desserts; it will keep, tightly sealed, for up to 1 year.

STOCK YOUR PANTRY

take inventory Remove everything from the pantry and sort the items by type. Take inventory of what you have using the Pantry Staples list (page 106).

clean wipe the shelves clean and reline them with shelf paper, if needed.

check freshness Look for expiration dates on all the items and discard anything that has passed its date. Also, throw away any items that have a stale or otherwise questionable appearance, odor, or flavor.

list & shop Make a list of all the items that you need to replace or buy, and then make a trip to the store to buy everything on your list.

restock Put all your pantry items away, organizing them as much as possible by type of ingredient so everything is easy to find. Place newer items behind older ones, so you'll use the older ones first. Keep staples that you use often toward the front of the pantry as well.

mark the date Write the date directly on the package of each new item before putting it away, so you'll know when you bought it and when to replace it.

KEEP IT ORGANIZED

review your recipes Look over the recipes you plan to make during the week to see what ingredients you'll need.

check your staples Take a look in your pantry to be sure you have the ingredients you'll need on hand.

make a list Draw up a list of any items that are missing, so you can replace them when you go shopping.

rotate items Mark the date on your new purchases, then place them in the pantry. As you put them away, check what you already have and rotate the items as needed, moving the oldest ones to the front so they will be used first.

OVENS

The recipes in this book were tested using a conventional oven. Any oven can have hot spots; also, large pans and baking sheets can block heat and create variances in temperature between racks.

To ensure the dessert you are baking cooks evenly, check occasionally and rotate the pans as needed. If you are baking two sheets of cookies at the same time, switch them between the oven racks and rotate the pans 180 degrees midway through baking.

An accurate oven temperature is important to successful desserts. Use an oven thermometer to make sure your oven is heating correctly.

■ **Flours & grains** Flours and whole grains require proper storage to prevent them from developing stale odors and flavors. Stored in an airtight container and kept in a cool, dry place, rolled oats will keep for up to 2 months. All-purpose (plain) flour and cake (soft-wheat) flour can also become stale over time, so buy no more than you will use in 6 months and store in airtight containers.

■ **Leavening agents** Baking powder, baking soda (bicarbonate of soda), and cream of tartar are chemical leaveners that interact with liquid or acidic ingredients in a batter to produce bubbles of carbon dioxide. As a cake or other dessert bakes, the bubbles expand, causing the batter to rise. Mark the date of purchase on the containers and store baking powder and baking soda for no more than 6 months and cream of tartar for no more than 1 year. (If you store a box of baking soda in the refrigerator to combat odors, keep a separate box in the pantry for baking.) To test if a leavener is still effective, scoop out a spoonful and add a little water to it. It should fizz vigorously.

■ **Sweeteners** Store all types of sugar in airtight containers. Brown sugar, which is granulated sugar that has been mixed with molasses to add flavor and give it a soft, packable consistency, hardens when exposed to air. If this happens, warm it gently in a low oven or a microwave until it softens. Powdered (icing) sugar is made from granulated sugar that has been milled until very fine and mixed with a small amount of cornstarch (cornflour) to prevent clumping. If lumps do form, pass it through a sieve. If honey crystallizes, stand the jar in a saucepan of warm water over low heat or warm in the microwave until it is a smooth and pourable liquid.

■ **Spirits** Buy good-quality spirits in small bottles. You never need more than a spoonful or two, and cheaper versions tend to taste harsh or contain artificial ingredients that impart an off flavor. A sprinkle of orange-scented Cointreau or almond-flavored amaretto can turn a simple fruit salad into an elegant dessert, especially when paired with homemade pound cake. Keep spirits stored tightly closed. They will keep indefinitely, but have the best flavor if used within 6 months.

PANTRY STAPLES

SWEETENERS

corn syrup

honey

maple syrup

sugar, dark brown

sugar, coarse

sugar, granulated

sugar, light brown

sugar, powdered (icing)

SPICES & FLAVORINGS

cinnamon, ground

cinnamon, stick

ginger, ground

nutmeg, ground

peppercorns

red chile, ground

salt

vanilla extract

NUTS & DRIED FRUITS

almonds, slivered

apples

coconut, sweetened shredded

coconut, unsweetened shredded

currants

dates

raisins

walnuts

LEAVENING AGENTS

baking powder

baking soda (bicarbonate of soda)

cream of tartar

FLOURS & GRAINS

cake (soft-wheat) flour

flour, unbleached all-purpose (plain)

oats, rolled

rice, long-grain white

CHOCOLATE & COCOA

chocolate, bittersweet

chocolate, semisweet (plain)

chocolate, unsweetened

cocoa powder, unsweetened

WINES & SPIRITS

brandy

orange liqueur such as Cointreau or Grand Marnier

dark rum

kirsch

raspberry liqueur

sweet white wine such as Riesling or Muscat

CANNED & JARRED FOODS

apricot jam

pumpkin purée

raspberry jam, seedless

sour cherries, pitted

MISCELLANEOUS

balsamic vinegar

chai tea

coffee, ground

ginger, crystallized

instant coffee powder

WEIGHTS & EQUIVALENTS

All-purpose (plain) flour, unsifted

¼ cup	1½ oz/45 g
⅓ cup	2 oz/60 g
½ cup	2½ oz/75 g
1 cup	5 oz/155 g

Granulated sugar

2 tablespoons	1 oz/30 g
3 tablespoons	1½ oz/45 g
¼ cup	2 oz/60 g
⅓ cup	3 oz/90 g
½ cup	4 oz/125 g
1 cup	8 oz/250 g

Brown sugar, firmly packed

¼ cup	2 oz/60 g
⅓ cup	2½ oz/75 g
½ cup	3½ oz/105 g
1 cup	7 oz/220 g

Butter

1 tablespoon	½ oz/15 g
2 tablespoons	1 oz/30 g
4 tablespoons	2 oz/60 g
⅓ cup	3 oz/90 g
½ cup	4 oz/125 g
1 cup	8 oz/250 g

cold storage

Once you have organized your pantry, you can apply the same principles to your refrigerator and freezer. Both are good for storing staples, plus they are used for chilling some baked goods and unbaked pastry and cookie dough (page 101).

general tips

- Remove items a few at a time and give the refrigerator and freezer a thorough cleaning with warm, soapy water.

- Discard old or questionable items.

- Use the Cold Storage Staples list (left) as a starting point to decide what you need to buy or replace.

- Keep your freezer below 0°F (-18°C), and avoid packing it too tightly. You want air to circulate freely, which helps preserve the flavor and texture of foods. To freeze foods, let cool to room temperature, pack in airtight containers, and label with the name and date. Thaw baked goods in the refrigerator, in a microwave, or at room temperature.

fruit storage

Depending on the season, you may have a variety of fruits on hand, either in the refrigerator or on the countertop. You can keep pears, peaches, plums, nectarines, and pineapples at room temperature to ripen and soften and then refrigerate them. Be sure to always store bananas at room temperature. Store other fruits, including apples and berries, in the crisper drawer of the refrigerator.

Berries and figs are particularly fragile, and should be used within a day or two of purchase. To prevent them from developing mold or bruising, line a shallow plastic container with a paper towel, top evenly with a single layer of unrinsed berries, cover tightly, and refrigerate; rinse just before using.

index

weldon**owen**

415 Jackson Street, Suite 200, San Francisco, CA 94111
www.wopublishing.com

MEALS IN MINUTES SERIES

Conceived and produced by Weldon Owen Inc.
Copyright © 2007 by Weldon Owen Inc. and Williams-Sonoma, Inc.

The recipes in this book have been previously published as *Desserts* in the Food Made Fast series.

Color separations by Mission Productions in China
Printed by 1010 Printing in China

Set in Formata
This edition first printed in 2011
10 9 8 7 6 5 4 3 2

Library of Congress Cataloging-in-Publication data is available.

Weldon Owen is a division of
BONNIER

Photographers Tucker & Hossler
Food Stylist Kevin Crafts
Food Stylist's Assistant Alexa Hyman
Text Writer Kate Chynoweth

ACKNOWLEDGMENTS

Weldon Owen wishes to thank the following people for their generous support in producing this book: Heather Belt, Ken DellaPenta, Judith Dunham, Peggy Fallon, Denise Lincoln, Emily Miller, Marianne Mitten, and Sharon Silva.

ISBN-13: 978-1-61628-215-8 (paperback)
ISBN-10: 1-61628-215-0

ISBN-13: 978-1-61628-172-4 (hardcover)
ISBN-10: 1-61628-172-3

A NOTE ON WEIGHTS AND MEASURES

All recipes include customary U.S. and metric measurements. Metric conversions are based on a standard developed for these books and have been rounded off. Actual weights may vary.